Are You a Happy Couple?
(A Handbook for Healthier Relationships, Whether Together or Apart)

I have been involved in therapeutic work with couples and children of divorce for over twenty-five years, having read much of what is out there in order to understand the issues, therapies, and interventions that are state-of-the-art. I tried my best to help couples to accept their differences and different perspectives, to determine why they came together initially. Some were too far along the road of hurt, anger, and resentment to return to what it was that brought them together. I was struck by the pain they felt, seeing a dream die for each couple and helped them grieve at the loss of something they created together. But it was the <u>children,</u> the unwilling victims who touched my heart the most, as they tried to make sense of the promise they felt their parents had made them about a family together, not divided. There was no "easy" age for this to happen to them and they felt betrayed by the people they had trusted the most.

This book is written for professionals, parents, and people contemplating or going through relationship turmoil, a separation or divorce. Anyone considering marriage and working through their relationship struggles would also benefit from a proactive approach to their relationship, to learn and address the critical components of a fundamentally healthy relationship. One can learn to love again, to be happy again, and be wiser and stronger, making sure to meet your individual needs, your children's needs, as well as your partner's needs. It's not a failure, it's a warm-up for better things ahead, but you've got some healing to do first and so do your children as they make their way out of the confusion and pain to develop a new relationship with each parent. We need to keep our eyes focused on the future, deal with the present and understand the past to help us realize that goal. Only you can understand you best, how you feel, what you've been through and what you want out of life. A therapist can only guide and help to steer you on your course, appreciating your strengths and challenging your weaknesses to achieve what your heart desires.

TABLE OF CONTENTS

1) Relationships: What do you really want from them?

2) Critical Components of a Healthy Relationship

3) What is marriage about, anyway?

4) So, you're having some problems: Communication with no surprises

5) Doing what it takes to make it work

6) Your financial goals together & how to achieve them.

7) Meeting emotional needs.

8) Intimacy & sexuality: Not necessarily the same thing.

9) Spirituality

10) You've tried it all and can't take it any longer (There's no "best" age for the kids to survive this best)

11) A child's perspective: Why are you ruining my life?

12) Pitfalls and traps that make matters worse: The blame-game

13) Focus on the children

14) The aftermath: Consolidation and growth

15) New relationships: Can you ever trust again?

Chapter 1: Relationships: What Do You Really Want From Them?

What do any of us want from people in our lives? We want to be loved, to be listened to, to share our joys, our sadness, our passions, the fun and the tough times. It begins with our very first relationship: with our parents, but the first face we see is our mother's. We've heard her heartbeat, felt her warmth, safe and secure in the luxury of a place where we are fed, sheltered, protected and feel loved. Then suddenly, we come out into a cold, noisy world where all we want is to feel the same things. I've always felt sad for babies when they first enter into this world. What a cruel shock it must be to suddenly see, hear, smell and feel things they have no idea how to cope with or to respond to. Babies are pre-programmed to be able to focus their eyes right at the focal point of their mother's face as she nurses them. That is where the trust begins, hopefully. They know her voice from hearing her inside. They see her face during those first crucial moments upon entering this world and feel the warmth of their body against hers. From a parent's perspective, it is literally love at first sight.

Fathers are definitely at a disadvantage in this respect, because they have to make themselves known since they haven't had the same physical connection to their growing infant. In the old days, before dads could be there for the birth, I can't imagine how stressful, scary and frustrating it must have been to have had to "walk the carpet" in the waiting room – not to be able to hear the first cry, to see that little face and count the little pink fingers and toes. Nowadays, sometimes dads are the first ones to get to hold their babies while the doctors and nurses are finishing things up with the new mom. Whether mother or father, one of the first promises we make to our little ones is that we will always be there for them, that they can trust us to protect them and we will love them no matter what. Then, they come home with us to sometimes endless sleepless nights – so helpless and dependent. All we can respond to is their cries: is it a wet diaper, a feeding or just a cuddle that they need? We try desperately to listen and understand, to meet their needs the best we can.

It's the unconditional love, the caring, the listening that we crave from the moment we enter this world until the day we leave it. I always tell young parents as they struggle to understand through bleary, sleep-deprived eyes that what their child needs and will always need is their love, no matter what. We may not always like them as we go through the struggles of toddler-hood, childhood, and the teenage years, but we will always love them. It's the misunderstandings, miscommunication, misbehavior, distrust, disrespect and dishonesty that get in the way of any relationship, whether parent-child, between siblings, or between parents. We want to be understood: how we feel, what we want what we need. We want to be able to listen and be listened to, not to have to show it through misbehavior. We want to be trusted and to be able to trust, to respect and be respected, to be honest and have others be honest with us. But sometimes, the patterns of our first relationships repeat themselves in our later lives.

Once infants begin to understand the relationship between their cries and their parents' behavior, they are starting to establish the trusting connection. Their cries are heard (or not) and their needs are respected and met (or not). They begin to develop a secure (or insecure) attachment or connection to their care-givers, whether it's their parents, their grand-parents, their foster-parents, aunts, uncles, or siblings. They are dependent upon that trust for their survival. If they are not heard or listened to, they may begin to expect that others will not meet their needs and cannot be trusted or don't love them.

And that is what they search for their whole lives, never really expecting that they'll find it.

Toddlers having a tantrum are confused with so many feelings, and only want to be understood. Helping them express how they feel and trying to understand it is the basis of how trust develops into the next phase of their lives. We continue to respect their needs without responding to every want. A tantrum to get what they want (like a candy-bar at a store) just reinforces that they can get whatever they want if they just scream loud enough. If their needs for food, warmth, comfort and love are met, we don't have to give in to every want.

Children's behavior (or misbehavior as it will sometimes be) is an attempt to get what they want. If they want comfort or companionship, food or attention, they will try to get it the right way (which we are supposed to reward) or the wrong way (which they'll try to do if their needs are consistently ignored). We try to teach them the right way, to exercise self-control and self-discipline, to earn their rewards and not just expect them, but if we're not consistent, they will eventually stop listening. They stop trusting us to do what we promised: to respect their needs, to show them that we will love them and take care of them.

One of my favorite children's books is by Robert Munsch, called "Love You Forever". I loved it so much, my children and I made up our own music for the refrain: "I'll love you for always, I'll like you forever, as long as I'm living, my baby you'll be...". I loved it so much, I bought copies for my mother and mother-in-law to read to my kids and my niece and tape it for them in their own voices, so that they could hear their grandmothers read them a bedtime story from provinces far away. The message is an age-old one: we will always be their parents, until the day that we die. In the book, after his mother dies, the grown-up son rocks his aged mother in his arms and sings to her: "I'll love you for always, I'll like you forever, as long as I'm living, my mother you'll be"…and so it continues on with his own infant. I still get tears in my eyes when I think of it and I still love singing it or reading it with my now grown children. They will always be our children and we will always be their parents. These are the ties that bind us together forever.

Before we know it, those dreaded teenage years come and we are no longer the apples of our children's eyes. Those trusting little faces that once asked us every question under the sun (and thought we knew the right answer) look at us like we're the stupidest creatures in the world. We don't know anything anymore. We don't understand, who cares if we've "been there, done that", the world is different now. We just don't "get it". As we reel from the dizzying heights of knowing everything to knowing nothing, we struggle with our own personal dilemmas. We want them to be good people, to be successful and happy, to find the right career, the right partner, make the right choices, to take care of themselves and exercise the self-control and self-discipline we taught them as children. Suddenly, the saying: "I'll always love you, but I don't always like you" comes to mind and it's mutual! They test the boundaries of trust, stretch the truth, push the limits of respect and the communication we so carefully nurtured becomes strained. Are they meeting their potential? Are they respecting themselves (and us)? Are they being true to themselves? Are they in relationships we want them to be in? Are they taking care of themselves like we taught them to? The existential crisis begins as they struggle to find who they are and where they belong in this world apart from us.

They, like us, are searching for meaning in their lives: we hope through succeeding in school and finding a career and a good group of friends and a life partner who cares about them as much as we do. And that is where "Romeo and Juliet" comes in. They want us to trust them, to listen to them, to respect their choices, and to try and understand. The more we may disagree, the more they are in love with the idea, the choice, the decision. It's the age-old "catch 22": if you say too much or disagree too strongly, they are driven away but if you say too little or nothing at all, they may do the wrong thing. The fundamental trust is shaken. We don't know everything, we can't always make them happy and safe and comforted, we don't always listen to what they think they need.

What are children looking for in relationships with people outside the family? They're looking for someone to have fun with, to play with, to be there when they want to do something or are bored or lonely. Teens are searching for understanding, people who listen to them and enjoy doing the same things. They're growing apart from us and searching elsewhere to fill the void. We are no longer the nucleus of their lives. They can hopefully trust that we're still there, but they start to look elsewhere to meet their needs. They search out others and start to "date" (an antiquated term, I'm told), hopefully narrowing down what it is they want or don't want in searching for a partner in their lives.

The age-old mating ritual begins and no matter what generation we're from, the competition between guys for girls seems so much less intense than between girls for guys. Teenage girl-friends can be incredibly mean as they battle (usually behind each other's backs) for the boys. The intensity of "best friends" among girls is challenged by the competition of their time together with their boyfriends. Sound familiar? It's no different today than in our day. The difference is that girls are more willing to fight for their boys physically than ever before. Our children do live in a "different world" than we remember. No, they don't "date", but they do "hang out" together, often "24/7", before, during and after school, well into the night over the phone if you don't watch it! I've tried to explain the concept of "dating" (boy, do I date myself when I do) and how we would wait by the window or the door to be picked up for an evening, perhaps calling each other once or twice during the week. Nowadays, young couples are around each other so much, I tell them they're like an old married couple after a couple of months together and get bored with each other.

Dating is about finding out what it is we want and what we don't want in a relationship with someone. If people don't date enough before they think they find "Mr. or Ms. Right", they often settle for someone to just not have to be alone. In the single world now, I watch and see people in bars at the end of the night, struggling to "pair-up", hoping it may be someone they have something in common with, someone to provide comfort in the bleak world of being alone. You can see the desperation in them as the bar gets ready to close and they see couples going off together. It's certainly rarely a place to meet your soul-mate, the person of your dreams. More successful matches seem to come from meeting people in clubs or groups with similar interests, whether it's a sport, an art class, a dance class, or a church group. There, at least, they have something in common as a starting point.

Therein lies the source of so many mismatches: people look to "complete" themselves with someone else, without completing themselves first. At a bar, people "blow off steam" after a week of work and want to have some fun. They have that in common, but what about other things? What about being able to share something they both have a passion for, other than finding someone to be with?

Relationships take time, to develop the trust, the caring, the respect, the honesty about themselves, to be able to communicate how they feel and what they want in life. These needs are no different than what they hopefully had with their parents. If they didn't have it, then they still search for it. How many times have we heard of women who end up with men like their fathers or men with women like their mothers? Sometimes it's a good thing, and sometimes it's really not.

The truth is, we all want to be loved for who we are. We want someone to care about us as much as we care about them. We want to be heard: how we feel, what we want and what we need. We want to be respected for who we are and what we do for ourselves and others. We want honesty, to be able to be honest without being blamed or judged for it and for our partner to be honest with us. We want to be able to trust that our potential partner in life will not purposefully hurt us but will listen to how we feel: what makes us feel good, what makes us happy, what hurts, what makes us sad. We want them to trust that we will do the same.

People talk about finding their "soul-mate", someone who can understand them without even having to talk, someone who sees them to the very core of their being and understands what is in their heart. In working with couples, I often talk about speaking from your "head" or your "heart" and this is what I mean, people who speak from the heart. Anyone can figure out a solution to a problem, but it takes that special person to be able to really understand how you feel, just to be there and not tell you what to do...to feel what you feel and share in the good times and the bad. Isn't that what the marriage vows are about? One of the promises is "In sickness and in health", to be able to share the happiness and the sadness in life, to shoulder the burdens together and love each other no matter what. They say that "two heads are better than one", but I believe that two hearts are better than one because that is where the love is, the compassion, the caring that we miss when we separate from our parents.

Falling in love is one thing and it feels great but keeping the love alive is another. That is about real dedication to another person, the maturity to put our own needs and feelings aside and **truly listen** and feel what another person feels. People want to be understood, to be loved for who they are, to be accepted, to be listened to and to be cared about no matter what. That is what we search for in our lives.

Chapter 2: Critical Components of a Healthy Relationship

In my work with couples, I find that they often come for counseling at the 10- and 20-year mark of being together. At ten years into a relationship, they most often have a child or children together and are beginning to lose themselves as individuals and as a couple. Many remain together "for the children" but have not allowed themselves to continue to grow as individuals or together as a couple, missing some critical components of what they needed to keep on doing. The 20-year point is often as the children are starting to leave home and the empty-nesters look at each other across the dinner table, wondering: "who are you, other than mom or dad?". Unfortunately, sometimes things are too far gone to find themselves again as individuals or as a couple to repair what they have lost. Luckily, often there is enough love and dedication there to have a solid foundation to work on together. It takes a lot of patience and compassion to help each other find their way. I feel truly blessed when I have the trust of these people to help them find themselves again.

Communication, honesty, respect and trust: those are the 4 components that make or break a relationship. It's as simple as that. If a couple had them at one time, they can regain them, but without regular maintenance and nurturance of each other, they start to disintegrate. Any inequities between two people, whether it's in a marriage, between parent and child, between children, between adult siblings, friends, coworkers, or between children and an authority figure, you name it, the imbalance causes problems. It takes recognition, caring and effort to maintain a healthy relationship. Let's look at how this "relationship box", with the components at the four corners keeping it strong and symmetrical is supposed to work. There has to be a balance between partners in a relationship on all 4 components, as well as stability within the relationship over time.

In order to begin a relationship with someone, there has to be **communication** or you would never have met in the first place. Communication is a sharing of ideas, feelings, thoughts, memories, and experiences, among other things. It can be verbal or non-verbal, through body-language or facial expressions. Think of when you met your significant other (or ex-) for the first time. How did you connect? What did you talk about? What did you get to know about them or what did they get to know about you at the beginning? How long did it take to really "get to know" each other? How much did you share about yourself?

Keeping up with communication/sharing is a never-ending process. Does anyone ever really know everything about us? Do they need to? Without proper, honest talk, miscommunication and assumptions arise that can lead to hurt, anger and built-up resentment. Years of not really listening but filtering another person's words through our own needs and perspective leads to detachment from each other. Why bother talking when it feels like no one is listening? The balance between talking and listening has to be maintained. More about communication later…

Honesty begins from the first communication with each other. It's about saying what we truly feel, what we really think, who we really are. First impressions count, and sometimes people "stretch the truth" in the beginning of a relationship in order to attract the other person (or not detract from themselves). This is to be expected, but to be a genuine person with someone else is to be the person you present yourself to be. Some of this depends upon where two people meet. If it's in a bar, chances are that the initial attraction is not to the person inside, because that's not what they see. If it lasts past the first flurry, it takes time to get to know someone. Relationships that start through work or mutual interests tend to give a clearer picture of the other person, that there are things in common already.

Does honesty mean sharing every nitty-gritty detail about our lives? Some people feel that some of their past is better left unsaid and could be perceived as "baggage" by the other person. Our past experiences have shaped and contributed to who we are, however, and would help explain how we feel and what we do. Whereas being honest or telling the truth about the past (which may come out anyway and result in feelings of betrayal if it comes from someone else) may depend upon how much the other person wants to hear, honesty about **feelings** is of paramount importance. There is no question that some people talk more from their heads than from their hearts, and when paired with each other, this mix of the two can spell disaster. If the heart/feelings person tries to express how they feel and it is intellectualized by the head/thoughts person, it can lead to serious feelings of being misunderstood. They almost speak in two different languages and practically need a translator.

Talking about what feels good that the other person is doing or has done, as well as what doesn't feel so good helps a relationship immeasurably. If this doesn't happen, resentments will build up. Let me give an example: after a couple has been together for many years, the wife comes home from grocery shopping, having gotten a sale on pasta. The husband sees what she has bought and berates her for buying spaghettini, which he apparently told her at some point he hasn't liked for all their years together. But he never told her, as far as she can remember. For him, it shows how little she cares what he likes and how he feels, how she "never listens". It's news to her, but the damage has been done, no matter how she tries to explain that she didn't know. We'll call this the "spaghettini fiasco" and refer back to it later.

Respect is such a misunderstood word. It means something different to everyone. When I work with teens and their parents, the word comes up constantly in that both want to be respected. In questioning further, however, it is often clear that it means different things to each of them. To parents, often respect means following house rules, no swearing or yelling at them and no name-calling. To teens, it often means giving them their privacy: not snooping in their email or phone messages, not reading their diaries or going into their rooms without asking first. They're using the same word to describe two different but complementary needs. The same goes for any relationship.

This is where we see how the other components inter-play. In order to have our needs respected, we have to effectively **communicate** them to the other person. We also have to be **honest** about how things make us feel so that we don't "set up" the other person to disrespect the needs we haven't effectively communicated. Respect is mutual in that there has to be a balance. People will respect those who they feel respect them.

We live in a different era than when I grew up, as like many of us, I was raised to "respect my elders" unconditionally, even if I felt that sometimes they didn't respect me. Giving people respect was unquestioned back then, yet I consistently hear from many teenagers that they'll give their parents respect when they feel that they're respected, not unconditionally. The same goes for other authority figures in their lives, like teachers: we were taught at home that we should respect our teachers and listen to what they wanted from us without question. The "earning respect" motto seems to have extended to kids in the classroom nowadays, because I have never seen more defiance of teachers ever. This creates its own share of problems. In any case, in any relationship, both parties need to feel respected by the other, to feel valued and worthy of being treated well. Any imbalance will result in resentment.

Finally, the fourth cornerstone of a healthy relationship is **trust.** Can we trust the other person's feelings, their intentions, their honesty? Can they be depended upon? This depends upon where a person comes from in previous relationships. If they've been lied to or cheated on, they're less likely to be trusting from the beginning. People come from different directions on this one. Some people give all of their trust in the beginning, "laying their cards on the table", "putting their hearts on their sleeve" and hoping that the other person also "bargains in good faith". Others feel that trust has to be earned and slowly share how they feel, what they've experienced, what they want and need. It's a slower process for them to "test the waters", to let the other person prove that they are worthy of greater trust.

Some would consider the first person, who gives trust unquestioningly, to be naïve. Yet, they are willing to take a chance and show "all of their cards", who they really are from the beginning because they believe that if they don't show who they really are, they may attract the wrong person. They take a big chance of being hurt. The second, more cautious individual is wary of being hurt and often feels that trust, like respect, has to be earned. While they may be less likely to be hurt earlier on in a relationship because they take their time to get to know someone and to show who they are, they may lose out as well. Who they show themselves to be may not attract the right person from the beginning and they may set themselves up for failure.

Any way you look at it, relationships are incredibly complex. There is so much going on, of what people are willing to show of themselves: what they want, what they need, how they feel, what they've been through. Communication is the key to being honest, to being able to trust and be trusted, to being respected. Love is only the beginning...

Chapter 3: What is Marriage about, Anyway?

Spring has sprung and we see so many engagement and wedding announcements in the newspaper. We see hordes of "stags" and "stagettes" at bars and other venues. We drive past loads of limousines with "just married" signs attached, numerous bridal retinues having their pictures taken at gardens and other vantage points in our cities. These happy couples have decided to take the next step to commit themselves to each other. What makes them think they're ready? Good question.

Marriage is supposed to be about a legal and spiritual commitment to another person. When a couple decide to "tie the knot", they have decided that they want to spend the rest of their lives together. Nowadays, with an almost 50% divorce rate, it's almost more like until they can't stand each other anymore. As easy as it seems to decide to get married, now it's easier to get "unmarried" than ever before. I am almost surprised when I speak to children or teens who tell me that their parents are still together. It takes work to establish and maintain a relationship, more than many starry-eyed newlyweds can even imagine.

In talking to couples who have been married a long time, they all agree that compromise is the key: listening to each other's feelings and needs and trying to meet them while still meeting their own individual needs. They talk about maintaining **intimacy**, not just the sexual kind, but a true and genuine connection, an almost unspoken understanding. They see disagreements not as potential conflict, arguments or fights, but as opportunities to work things out, to discuss and listen to each other. They are willing to really listen to what the other person has to say, not as a jumping-off point to prove their point. It is truly about respecting another person, their needs, their wants, their values, their feelings. It's not just in the moment of "being in love", it really means the age old vow: "in sickness and in health"…in good times and bad. That's what makes a marriage into a couple who work together for themselves and for each other. When one feels happy and successful, good about himself or herself, the other should be able to feel the same way. What is for the good of one is for the good of them both…like the "Three Musketeers", only it's two and then this adds on as the family grows, working together. All for one and one for all…

So much has to discussed and understood before a couple decides to unite: what has made them happy, what has made them sad, what they want out of life, their hopes, and their dreams for the future. It's not about the giddiness about feeling in love because that's not enough to sustain them. They have to be willing to **accept** each other and not expect the other person to change for them. No one will willingly change for another person without feeling some resentment. People will grow and change on their own and there needs to be openness and understanding as they do. They, in turn have to be willing to listen to and understand feedback from those around them.

Too many couples have admitted to me that from the beginning of their relationship, there were things that they didn't like about the other person, but they thought it would change over time or it wouldn't bother them. Yet it often does still bother them. It's important to never expect that, never assume to know someone better than they know themselves or you'll be disappointed. There will be surprises, some good and some bad, but that has to be expected.

Some couples think that living together before marriage will tell them what they need to know about someone: if they're compatible and can live together successfully. There is still a "honeymoon period", however, when people are on their best behavior. For some, it lasts longer than others. I've been amazed at some couples who have lived together for years before getting married and somehow, marriage changes the relationship. Some live together for life without ever getting formally married and stay happy together. They feel as committed to each other as any married couple.

It all comes down to being willing to work together for a common goal, a shared dream. For some, it's about owning a home together and financial security, for others it's about having a family, for others it's about saving for their retirement together, to be able to golf or travel together. They need to be on the same page, whatever they choose to dream about. It's about mutual support in their careers, and with each other's families and friends.

How much do you need to know about someone to feel you can trust them and feel respected by them enough to live your life together? How much do you have to be able to agree or compromise to know that you're going to make it? It's different for everyone. Some of the tolerance for another person's issues or differences depends upon our own experience in previous relationships and what we have seen from our parents', our relatives', or our friends' relationships. If a person has been "burned before" by a spouse cheating or lots of conflict, he or she is probably going to have a hard time accepting a relationship with much fighting or conflict. That's where sharing past experiences and expectations needs to come into play. Again, being honest about what bothers someone in a relationship needs to be dealt with as soon as it shows up.

Whether a person has experienced a less-than-ideal relationship before firsthand, or seen it in their parents' or other marriages, often the "warning bells" go on and it gets ignored. Falling in love and staying in love are two different things. It's the starry-eyes and breathless anticipation of every moment together that often gets in the way of people's judgment. When patterns start repeating themselves with hurt feelings and accusations, sometimes it's too late to fix the situation. Being clear in what you want, how you feel and what you need from someone must be kept foremost in your mind from day one. The more a person says and asks, the better. That way there are no illusions.

Did I say before that marriage is hard work? That, and being a parent are about the hardest jobs a person can take on. It takes dedication and commitment to work it through, to keep on the same page of what you both want and need. Never second-guess, always check out assumptions before blaming and accusing. When people tell me that their parents never argued and that's the bar they are holding their relationship up to, I tell them that it's unrealistic. How else can two individuals, who come from different families, different lives, different experiences ever hope to get along? It's all in the way you handle disagreements, respectfully hearing the other person out and feeling respected enough to express what you have to say.

When it comes to marriage, the more you know about each other better. The longer you've known each other, the better. The couples who've been through a lot together and seen each other during the tough times have fewer illusions of perfection. They've seen each other at their worst. Two individuals who want to be together and can see the strength of a life lived together, without needing the other person to survive will be stronger as a couple. They maintain themselves as individuals but have a healthy **inter-dependence** rather than a **dependence** upon each other. They can stand alone but want more out of life that they can see happening with another person who shares their goals and their dreams. They don't need to be together but want to be together.

Chapter 4: So, You're Having Some Problems: Communication with No Surprises

I've already talked about how crucial communication is for a healthy relationship. What does that mean? It means being honest and upfront with each other about what works and what doesn't work. It means sharing the good with the bad ("in sickness and in health", remember the vows?). By the time a couple has realized they're having problems, usually much that they're communicating is conflict through arguing. Their underlying dissatisfaction impacts on everything, resulting in misinterpretation and assumptions constantly being made. Learning to communicate is no longer a pro-active exercise because everything is reactive.

So how do you stop the cycle of blame? The first step is to **stop**…stop reacting to the present, because it's highly emotionally driven by the past. It's time to take stock of what has happened, what your hopes and dreams were, what brought you together. The present feeds into the past, so everything has to be on the table. Start at the beginning, with when you first met…what attracted you to each other? How did you both look, what were you wearing, what were you doing, what was your first impression? There must have been something that attracted you to each other, for more than a first look! What was dating like, do you remember your first date, your first talk, your first kiss? What did you enjoy doing together? How was the romance/intimacy? Did you talk about your hopes and dreams for a future together? Can you remember what you each said? Take yourselves out of the day-to-day grind of today and remember when…it so easily gets forgotten. Remember how you used to talk?

When did you decide to marry? How did he/she propose? Do you remember preparations for the wedding? How about the stag/stagette/shower? About the wedding, do you remember how you both looked and felt? Where was the honeymoon, can you remember how you both felt? What was your first apartment/home together like? Do you remember decorating it, buying furniture together? Remember thinking about having your first child and then finding out you were pregnant? How did you both feel? Put together your memories of the birth of your first child...remember the excitement, the anxiety, the joy?! What did you do on anniversaries, birthdays, holidays? What about the good times with the kids, the shared family moments, the shared "stolen moments" as a couple?

We get so caught up in the stresses of everyday life that we forget the good times, as well as the stresses that we have made it through together. It can't have been all bad! How have you communicated as a couple before, other than through arguing? Is it emotional or intellectual? How have you connected before? Could you talk about feelings as well as thoughts, attitudes, hopes, dreams for the future? Were you ever on the "same page"?

Where and when were your best times to talk? Was it in bed at night, going through the day before falling asleep? Was it at breakfast in the morning as you have coffee together? Was it Saturday mornings sharing time together while the kids were watching cartoons? Was it on nights out, having the kids' babysat while you had an intimate dinner together? Was it lunch-hour chats as you both had lunch at work? There must have been times when you connected, to make some of the decisions you have had to in your life together up to this time...

How has life changed you both? Have your careers/ the kids changed you? Has extended family (out-laws/in-laws) been supportive or have they complicated things? What about friends, both couple- and individual? Do they cheer you on or do they serve to divide you? No one is the same as before, and that's okay because change and growth is a natural part of life. Now, it's about keeping in touch with the people you have both become.

Where did the resentments begin? Was it about jobs, extended family, finances, couple-time, leisure time, house-work sharing, kid-time, that caused upsets? Are you both happy in your careers, do you share your days with each other? Can you hear each other out without trying to "fix" things? Is extended family interfering with your own family-time or dynamic? Are you on the same page with regards to finances, savings, mortgages and other debt? Do you make time for each other as a couple? Do you share interests and experiences together? Do you help make time for each other to have individual friends and interests? Are you both satisfied that there is a fair sharing of family duties? Do you both contribute to and make time to share with the kids? These are all areas of potential conflict and aggravation and sometimes financial stress is the "straw that broke the camel's back" that can contribute to the downfall of a family equilibrium.

It's time to take stock of what you've accomplished together and to honestly work through what bothers you both. Never lose sight of having made it up to this point together. This is where real listening is important. Even if some things can't be changed, understanding what troubles our partner-in-life is a huge step towards showing that we still care. If, for instance, one of you is really unhappy in your job, can you work out a plan together that can make it better, to support the other? Maybe even just making time at the end of the day to work it through, perhaps problem-solve to make the situation better or look at other options brings some hope and a sharing of the burden.

Issues with extended family can complicate things because of divided loyalties. Although we care about our partner, we still care about our family-of-origin and sometimes the two can and will collide, trying to make everyone happy. Who you've married is who you've chosen to spend your life with. Isn't their happiness important, as it impacts on your own, as well? Is there a way to make things better, to listen to how extended family impacts and perhaps creates conflict, to help everyone get along? At the end of the day, you go home to each other and that is where compromise and support is important when it comes to dealings with extended family.

As we all know, financial stress hits us at the core of our being. It puts people in survival-mode in the struggle to make ends meet. Are you both in on a plan together to make your finances work? Do you have an end goal of paying off a mortgage, paying off debt, paying for kids' education, when and how you want to retire? Is one of you more invested in the future and saving for it while the other is more current-focused, spending as they go? Is there a way to accommodate both, to make both of you reasonably happy? Working together on your goals, seeing yourselves moving in a positive direction is a huge boost to your strength as a couple.

Do you take time to be together, whether in more formal "dates" or in "stolen moments", apart from the kids? It is very easy to lose sight of each other apart from being parents, wage-earners, soccer-moms, hockey-dads, house-keepers, gardeners, among so many other hats we wear. When was the last time you sat down and talked about each other, not about the kids, the jobs, the finances, the news, politics? What about the fascinating and intriguing things that drew you to each other in the first place? Do you still remember them? Have they changed or taken a back-seat? Can you still talk about how you feel, what you really want, what you need? This is the person you chose to spend your life with…isn't it important to still know them, for them to still know you? As busy as our schedules are, taking or making that time is crucial for the continued nurturance of yourselves as a couple.

Leisure-time is hard to come by with all of the pressures of today's world and busy families. Do you share things you enjoy together? Like doing puzzles or gardening or renovating together, joining a co-ed volleyball league or taking golf lessons together, taking ballroom dancing lessons together, going on walks with the family dog? Of course, so much depends upon kids' ages and accessibility to or need for babysitting…and then are the individual needs for time with friends in activities you enjoy. Moms-nights-out or watching the football game at friends'…do you give each other the time to do those things? Do you honestly support your partner to have fun on their own or with friends? These are essential breaks that allow each of us to recharge our batteries, to still be people in our own right.

Is there a fair sharing of house-hold responsibilities? Was this agreed upon when you got together, or has it changed with the addition of more to do, the addition of kids, of changes in work schedules? This is another potentially big source of resentment, if one partner feels that the burden of work with home and the family is upon them. Can you compromise, shift and share duties so that it feels more equal and less exhausting for one? Are you willing to do what it takes to make sure you both happier (understanding that a happier mate makes for a happier marriage)?

Are you on the same page when it comes to the kids? Do you both help out? Do you both spend time with them? Do you make enough time for family things? Do you agree and support each other in child-rearing and discipline? Do you agree about their schools, their outside activities, helping out and attending what you both can in the kids' outside endeavors, like going to practices, taking them to classes, watching games or recitals, helping with equipment and costumes? If not, can things be shifted, schedules be moved around to be a part of things more? Sharing the joy of our kids' lives and experiences only serves to bring a family even closer...This only a small list of the issues that can cause stress, conflict and tension in a marriage. Now onto how to better understand them and make it work...

Chapter 5: Doing What it Takes to Make it Work

In the last chapter, I talked about taking stock together of where you've come from, how you both feel things are going, and where you each want to see things going for the future. Instead of making you refer to an appendix at the back of the book, I'm providing you here with a directed set of questions to ask yourselves and each other to complete and share with each other. The first (*Where we've come from*), helps you to acknowledge your past together and remember why you came together in the first place. It is open-ended, with no ratings, only suggestions to jog your memories about the early years. The second (*Where we're at*), looks at how you feel the relationship stands in terms of the Four Cornerstones, areas of stress and strain. The third (*Where we're going*), focuses on what your goals are as an individual, as a couple, and as a family. The last two are rated from 1 to 5. The idea is to complete each of them on your own and then bring them together, to share and discuss your answers.

Be honest! Now is the time to really get to the nitty-gritty, to see what you have managed to accomplish together, if your needs are being met, if you still have the same vision for your future together...

Doing this, in itself, means that you are engaged in the process of trying to work things out, that it is important to you both. If some of the answers need more explanation that you want to remember, put an asterisk (*) beside the question and follow it up with some points on the back of the page...or write it up separately.

I often find that having couples write each other letters is a useful enterprise, sometimes better than engaging in the face-to-face conflict or arguments that only serve to divide them further. Writing up how you feel, what you want and need allows a person the time to really understand it for themselves. For your partner to take the time to read it, not to interject when they disagree, gives each a better chance to be heard and to feel respected.

Remember that no one can tell us how to feel or what to think. It is based on our own past experiences and everyone's is different. Show your partner the respect and appreciation for their honesty and sincere attempts to be understood. Each of you deserves it.

This is just a beginning, to open up the lines of communication and promote understanding. I would love to see you get together on a regular basis for this shared time to really feel you can express how you feel and think things are going and to really listen to what your partner is saying.

Questionnaire 1: Where We've Come From:

(Every relationship is different. These questions may all apply to you or some may not. Answer those that fit with the progression of your relationship through the years.)

1) What do you remember about the time you first met? What was your first impression? What was he/she wearing? Who were they with?

2) What was your first "date" like? Where did you go and what did you do? Do you remember what you talked about? Do you remember your first kiss?

3) How did things progress…when did you know that you had fallen in love?

4) What made you think that this was the person you wanted to spend your life with?

5) What did friends/family say?

6) Think about when you got engaged, remember the feelings…can you remember the details?

7) What about the plans for the wedding? Can you remember some specifics?

8) Did you have a stag/stagette/bachelor/bachelorette party? How did that go?

9) What do you remember about the wedding day? How did you feel?

10) Think about the honeymoon…what do you remember?

11) How was life living together in the beginning?

12) What about your first jobs when you got together, what were they like?

13) Think of your first place…what do you remember about it?

14) The decision to have children (or not)…what do you remember about it?

15) The birth of your first child (and subsequent others)…what memories do you have?

16) Think about family holidays together, whether at-home or away…what do you remember about them?

17) What do you remember of your anniversaries and other special moments together?

Questionnaire 2: Where We're At

Each question is rated from 1 to 5…
1 is Not at All, 2 is Somewhat, 3 is Okay, 4 is Pretty Good, 5 is Really Good.

1) I feel respected by my partner.   ____

2) I respect my partner.   ____

3) I feel trusted by my partner.   ____

4) I feel I can trust my partner.   ____

5) I am honest with my partner.   ____

6) I feel my partner is honest with me.   ____

7) I can communicate with my partner.   ____

8) My partner communicates with me.   ____

9) I feel my partner listens to me.   ____

10) I listen to my partner.   ____

11) I am happy in my job/career   ____

12) My partner is happy in her/his job/career ____

13) I am satisfied with our relationships with extended family.   ____

14) My partner is satisfied with our relationships with extended family.   ____

15) I am satisfied with how we manage our finances. ___

16) My partner is satisfied with how we manage our finances. ___

17) I feel we have enough couple-time together. ___

18) My partner feels that we have enough couple-time together. ___

19) I have enough time to myself. ___

20) My partner has enough time to him/herself. ___

21) I feel that we share household/family duties fairly. ___

22) My partner shares household/family duties fairly. ___

23) I feel that I spend enough time with our kids. ___

24) My partner spends enough time with our kids. ___

25) I feel that we share enough intimate time together. ___

26) My partner feels that we share enough intimate time together. ___

27) I am satisfied with our relationship. ___

28) My partner is satisfied with our relationship. ___

29) I am happy in our relationship. ___

30) My partner is happy in our relationship. ___

Questionnaire 3: Where We're Going

Again, rated 1 to 5…
1 is Not At All, 2 is Somewhat, 3 is Okay, 4 is Pretty Good, 5 is Really Good

1) We are on the same page in each of our career goals. ___

2) We have the same expectations of our extended families. ___

3) We have the same drive to spend time together as a couple. ___

4) We support each other's needs to spend time on our own. ___

5) We adjust and continue to accommodate sharing of duties. ___

6) We both see a continued need to spend time with our kids. ___

7) We have discussed our plans for retirement. ___

8) We know where we want to be when we are empty-nesters. ___

9) I can see us growing old together. ___

10) We are working towards our future together. ___

11) I want our kids to see us as role-models for their relationships. ___

12) We have the same financial goals. ___

13) We have the same goals for our family's spiritual life. ___

14) We have the same goals for our emotional relationship. ___

15) We have the same goals for our physical relationship. ___

So now, having completed the questionnaires, take the time to sit down with each other and share your answers one at a time. It's probably best not to do all 3 at once. Perhaps the first opportunity is just to focus on your shared past. You can trade papers and ask for feedback or read your answers to each other. Don't be frustrated with things that you may remember and your partner doesn't. The goal here is to bring back those good feelings and remember that some details may be more vivid for one of you than the other. That's okay. The point is that you went through these experiences together to take you to where you are now. Each step must have been worth it, because you kept on going!!!

For *Where We're At*, spend some time focusing on the first 10 that examine the 4 Cornerstones. Ask questions and be specific about what your partner does for you to feel that way. Let them know what works, too!!! Sometimes, people aren't aware of what they do right. With knowing it works or feels good, they are more motivated to do it more. With knowing what doesn't work or doesn't feel good, they can know better the impact of their words and actions.

The next set of questions in the second questionnaire examines more closely the specific elements of potential satisfaction or dissatisfaction in a relationship. No one will get an A+ in each one, so don't be worried. It's all a starting point to work better together.

The final questionnaire, looking at the future, is jumbled together on purpose. Financial, emotional, physical, and spiritual needs are all addressed here. Take a look at the overall lay-out of your answers…is one area more out-of-sync than another? Are you doing well, from both of your estimation, in one or a number of them? Then acknowledge that and pat each other and yourselves on the back…even with being 2 individuals, you have still been working together!

Now look at each of the specific areas. If you're not meeting mutual financial goals, look at how you can work together better to achieve them, and both be satisfied. If you or both of you don't feel emotionally nurtured in the relationship, focus on how you can better meet each other's needs. If your physical relationship needs some fine-tuning, talk about what feels good, what could feel even better. Is it the frequency or the quality of your intimacy that is missing? If your and your family's spiritual needs are not being met, talk through what could make it better and put that plan into action. More about each of these now…

Chapter 6: Our Financial Goals Together & How to Achieve Them

First off, understand that I am not a financial advisor. If you have one, work with them. If you don't, it may be a good idea to get one. They can provide a good, balanced perspective on realistic goals and how you can work together to meet them. What I am looking at here is the nuts-and-bolts of daily living, of saving and spending, the realities of the financial insecurity of our current times. No one is immune to whatever we want to call it…inflation, recession, keeping up with the cost of living and (hopefully) ahead of it.

When you got together, did you have similar spending or saving habits? Was one of you a dedicated "saver"? Was one of you just surviving pay-cheque-to-pay-cheque, a dedicated "spender"? If so, how did you manage to work things out before? Did you ever, or have you both just accepted your differences? With the financial crunch of being home-owners and/or parents, there just seems to be so much more to have to spend on, to have to save for…

Are you satisfied that your mutual earnings should be "enough" to make it work? Is one of you having to sacrifice? Are you both having to sacrifice together to make ends meet? Those stresses and strains of delaying what you want to do together, while difficult, make you a dedicated team working towards a greater goal together. It doesn't make it so tough to endure, inching towards being able to pay off your mortgage or pay off your debt or save for a family holiday or the kids' education. You have a clear vision of what you want to accomplish together and are willing to support each other to achieve it.

The difficulty seems to be when one member of the "team" doesn't seem to be as dedicated to the end-result. They can't seem to "delay gratification" for themselves, resulting in resentment by the teamplayer who is making personal sacrifices. Let's get specific here...I'm talking here about the one who goes on a splurge of shopping and racks up the credit card while the other is scrimping to make ends meet. It doesn't have to be that extreme, maybe happening occasionally or to a smaller extent, but the impact is still there on the bottom line.

Remember, we all come from different family backgrounds with different saving and spending histories. Some people follow their family pattern and others choose not to, choosing to create a different path for themselves. Putting those two individuals with different histories and individual financial habits together can create any multitude of scenarios.

Are you on the same page? If not, were you ever? If so, what changed? If you're on the same page, make sure to congratulate yourselves and each other. You're managed to figure out together a big piece of the healthy family puzzle. If you're not, read on...

If you were working together towards financial goals before, what turn-of-events changed that? Did something happen to make someone go off the agreed-upon path? Did a career change/job loss/family loss cause such a difference? Did the current economic climate make what worked before not work so well at some point? In other words, did "little expenditures" not affect the bottom-line before, but they do now?

Be honest with each other about what you see happening and what you think needs to happen. Understand that there is always room to work back towards your goals and again. A financial advisor will be able to help with the process. Don't be afraid to reach out to people who are professional at this before it is too late. Be kind to each other, to be willing to accommodate your partner's needs, that always having to "give in" for the greater good is tough. Acknowledge the sacrifices one partner may have made, even if you didn't ask them to.

What if you've never had a shared financial goal and have always gone off as individuals, doing your own thing financially? You are still connected at the bottom line unless your finances are totally separate. Is everything still getting paid?

It's obviously really important to see what your regular expenditures are on a monthly basis. Taking a look at what your costs are for rent or mortgage, heating, electricity, water, property taxes, insurance, cars, food, phones and internet, entertainment, credit cards (and that may not be an exhaustive list) is critical. Are they getting paid, how and by whom? Are they getting paid on time or late (causing extra fees for late-charges and potential impact on credit scores)?

When was it decided who was to handle paying bills, or do you just "play it by ear" as to who does it? Sometimes the one who has that responsibility tires of it or may not want to do it anymore. Or, they may not be the best for the job...switching this task can sometimes bring more drive to get this accomplished.

Both of you being aware of due-dates, institutions where bills are paid, outstanding expenses, overall debt and savings really helps. Nevertheless, connecting on a monthly basis as to where you're at financially, what has been paid and/or needs to be, where (if at all) spending habits need to be curbed or changed. Even having bill payment dates written on the monthly calendar and then crossed off as they are paid can help to maintain you on the same financial road. It could even be a shared job as in one picking up the mail and aligning the bills in order of date so that the other can pay them, then the paid bills (annotated with dates paid and reference numbers) being filed by the other. It doesn't have to be daunting. But those are the mechanics of keeping up with necessary expenses…what about if you disagree with expenditures?

Fixed expenses are just that…wherever you live, having decided to rent or buy, whatever size of home and amenities, utilities and regular living expenses must be paid. What if over-spending by one of you puts your ability to keep up in jeopardy? Honest communication about worries, fears or anxieties is critical here. It is always possible to re-align things, but it takes real listening to each other's perspectives and reasoning to work it through.

Obviously, financial stress hits us at the core of our being…being able to survive in our home, in our lifestyle. Are you both invested in your shared lifestyle, in your home? Have priorities shifted for one of you, so that you have other areas you want to spend on or save towards? For example, both of you may have gotten together in your jobs/careers and one or both may have decided to do a career change requiring further education or to open up a business. This is a mutual decision that impacts on your financial livelihood as a couple and a family. Adjustments and compromises obviously have to be made in order to keep up with just one regular pay-cheque, while the other's business or further education results in a regular income down the road.

The above scenario is a couple-decision working towards making things better for the family in the long run. But what if one member of the couple continues to spend beyond both their means, jeopardizing their shared livelihood? Something has to be done to equalize things, so that they see the impact on everyone. This is a tricky situation rife with resentments from the "saver" and potential entitlement by the "spender". If compromise and accommodation don't happen, it may be that the incomes need to be separated and regular payments for ½ of expenses and a certain (agreed-upon) amount of savings needs to come off the "spender's" account to ensure that things get paid. Whatever they have left is what doesn't impact on the family survival to spend. It seems radical but may be the only way to do damage control for everyone else.

At the end of the day, as in every other aspect of a relationship, communication is critical: saying how you feel, what you want and what you need. Being honest with each other about financial concerns or worries and being able to trust each other to accomplish your goals has to happen. Respecting how you each feel and feeling respected for what you do to accomplish these goals is important to work together as a team. After all, in the business of being a couple, of being a family, isn't good financial sense and health important?

Chapter 7: Meeting Emotional Needs

Just what are "emotional needs"? What do you need from each other emotionally to feel good about yourself and about each other? Everyone is different and knowing each other is so important to be able to answer that. What makes you happy? What makes your partner happy? What is really upsetting to you? What is really upsetting to your partner? There are so many emotions of so many colors and hues that they more than fill up a box of crayons.

First off, it's important to be able to know and express how you feel. Think about it: if even you don't know, how can your partner ever hope to know? Can you sit down and talk about how each of you feels, what feels bad, what feels good? Can you do it without saying "you make me feel...", instead saying "when you do this, I feel..."? Remember...no one can make us feel any way. How we respond or feel depends upon how we interpret it.

Can you "read" your partner from their facial expressions or body language? Do you know each other that well? Is it possible that you each make assumptions based on past experience with each other that may not be right? Let's take a scenario that stems from misinterpretation...

Say a wife comes home from work with a frustrated or angry look on her face and proceeds to go to the bedroom without speaking. The husband "knows" that look and stays away, giving her space, thinking he may have done something wrong. In actual fact, she may have had a bad day at work or a stressful drive or commute home and just wants some time to de-stress. There is nothing that the husband has done wrong, but he stays away, waiting until she comes out. Meanwhile, she is puzzled, waiting for him to join her so they can share tales of their days. She begins to feel either angry at being ignored or hurt that he doesn't seem to care. And so the assumptions continue until someone talks…

This is where even a little communication can go a long way towards a happier evening. It may take as much as the wife saying in passing: "I had a fight with a co-worker today, just need to change and get into the bath. Want to come join me later?". Or perhaps an implicit, pre-arranged mutual plan to give each other a 15-minute break when you get home from work, then to join one another is all it takes…

I am forever amazed at the couples I have worked with through the years, some married over 20 years, who don't either express what makes them happy or know what makes their partner happy. Take, for instance, how each person shows that they care about each other…he faithfully bathes the kids before bed and does the dishes after dinner and that is how he shows he cares. She acknowledges the team effort, but really just wants a hug when he gets home from work and a kiss before he leaves. Everyone has different ways they show love or caring and different ways they want to have it shown to them.

For some, giving or receiving gifts or tokens show affection. For others, mere physical touch like a hug or a kiss, holding hands or a shoulder squeeze shows they care. Some people prefer to be told they are loved on a regular basis. Yet others appreciate little things being done for them or doing things for others, like making the morning coffee or making the bed. Some people appreciate any combination of the above. Knowing and expressing what works for you and what makes your partner feel cared about is really important to maintain that emotional connection, the reason you came together in the first place.

I am a big fan of "stolen moments" that I encourage couples to eke out of their busy schedules. It might be a quick snuggle in the pantry while making dinner together, a sneaky kiss while doing laundry, a few moments to chat while the kids are napping, a quick call to say "I miss you, how are you doing?" over lunch hour at work, but every one counts. It is too easy to take each other for granted in our busy lives and only hope to plan for a "date" maybe every month, when you often just end up talking about the kids anyways.

As much as the buzz-phrase today is to "book in time" for ourselves to work out or meet friends, it is equally as important to fit in time for each other as a couple. It may be as simple as turning off the television and laptops when you get into bed at night and have a regular "connection time" at the end of the day. It could be a lunch out together once a week from work. It could be brunch out together while the kids are in a weekend class or sport. But it needs to happen, because time goes by, kids get older and move out and then at the end of the years together, who wants to sit across from each other and not know anything about that person other than they're "mom" or "dad"?

It's as simple as making and taking the time to still make yourselves a priority, because after all, didn't you start out as a couple, two individuals who made a life together? Don't you want to be happy? Don't you want your partner to be happy? Don't you want to be able to say what upsets/frustrates/angers or hurts you? Don't you want your partner to care and don't they want you to care?

Maybe it takes writing little notes or emails to each other to stay connected. Some people are far better at expressing themselves in written form than face-to-face…and letter-writing can give you each the chance to say how you feel without feeling judged or minimized. Sometimes the respect accorded with reading a letter or note, rather than reacting face-to-face gives the time to digest and understand. Sometimes taking the time to write how we feel allows us to clarify all of the emotions and explains it better for *ourselves*.

We should care about how our partner feels, because they're the person we chose to spend our lives with. It also impacts on us. Being able to hear: "when you do this, I feel…" allows us to understand, empathize and adjust. It gives the opportunity to make positive changes that make our partner feel better. Letting each other know what feels good is as important, because if we love someone, wouldn't we want to continue doing what helps them feel good?

Chapter 8: Intimacy & Sexuality: Not necessarily the same thing

When people hear the word "intimacy", many immediately assume it means sexuality. Yet, sex may not involve intimacy and intimacy may not involve sex. Interesting, isn't it? Intimacy is all about closeness, whether emotional, spiritual, or physical. It's about feeling safe enough to share and not be judged. Certainly, (and arguably) the best sex is with intimacy for women.

The sex drive or need for sex may not be equal between a couple. This discrepancy between the two can cause frustration for both: for the partner with a lower sex drive, they may feel pressured to have sex more often. For the partner who wants sex more often, he or she may feel resentful if their needs are not met. Again, we come to the need for communication.

The running stereotypical joke is for husbands to complain that their wives are not receptive to having sex as often as they would like. Similarly, the running joke with women is that they have had to become very adept at faking orgasms to please their husbands.

There has been a tremendous amount of research and writing about differing sex drives, sexual needs and the impact of hormonal differences between men and women. Similarly, the changes that happen throughout the life-span in each individual have been well-documented: for some, the drive reduces over time, for others it increases. None of it is predictable, but it makes sense to assume that two individuals in a relationship together will not necessarily go through changes at the same time. There will be disparities. The sexual relationship between a couple will go through "highs" and "lows" over time, depending upon outside factors (like stresses) and internal factors (like health, the overall relationship). It takes honesty, trust and perseverance to work it through.

Communication between a couple about not just frequency but quality of their sex life helps to maintain the closeness and openness between them. Being able to talk about what feels good, what you don't like, what you'd like to do and feel more requires a belief that you will be listened to and respected. What may have worked before may not feel so good anymore with bodily changes, health issues, child-birth, body image issues, among others. Feeling safe to talk about it is critical to maintaining a healthy and happy sex life.

Sometimes a lack of frequency may be because you're both so tired from your busy days with careers, kids and the home. It may be as simple as accommodating your schedule to fit in "quickies" during alone time when the kids are at activities or play-dates, or on a weekend morning when the kids are old enough to watch cartoons and make themselves breakfast. Maybe you can both work through a lunch-hour to be able to leave work early and get some alone time before the kids are home from school? We all know it takes creativity to keep things interesting sexually in long-term relationships.

It is a challenge to find the time, and the creativity to fit it in can make things interesting and even exciting. Some couples find that their sexual relationship has become "humdrum", boring or too predictable. Again, this is where communication and creativity, openness to trying new things can make all the difference. For some, a trip to a "sex shop" can result in some intriguing options, perhaps to bring some new excitement into their sex life. It is all about feeling safe, respected and not judged, however.

Just like "respect" can have very different meanings for different people, the same goes for "romance". Wine, roses, soft music, soft lighting, a wonderful meal can go a long way to setting the mood for more to come, but that may not work for everyone. A hot bath with candles surrounding the tub can set the stage for a relaxing, romantic romp. For some people, a hidden isolated hideaway like on a nature hike in a forest can do the trick. Only your imagination limits you.

So, what if your differences seem too much? Can you start again and learn about each other sexually at this time of your life? Of course, but it takes patience, trust and respect to break old patterns and old resentments that may have built up over time. I often suggest to couples that they set the stage with romance and closeness, an intimate setting and then don't follow up with making love. The expectation that sex has to follow from intimacy with each other often puts too much pressure to get through the setting to the act. Being able to cuddle, hug, talk and perhaps kiss without ending in sex can sometimes be as, if not more satisfying than ending up having sex. It also helps to build greater trust for the partner who feels that the expectation is always to end up having sex.

Making it playful, fun, no-pressure eases the seriousness that people attribute to having sex. Taking the time to listen and know each other's bodies again is well worth it. Celebrate the changes in each other's bodies, savor the delight of the special secret spots that drive each other wild. Make it an occasion with fore-play that can only further heighten the excitement for each other and end it with soft talk and snuggling, falling asleep in each other's arms. We know that for some, "getting going" without fore-play is too fast and leaves them hanging and for others, having your partner fall asleep afterwards while you want to revel in the after-glow of the moment is a let-down. Really, if you truly love each other, is it too much to ask to take your time? That is what really making love is all about…

And then there are the "quickies", when time is short…is there anything wrong with them? Not at all, as long as both partners are happy with it. What if only one partner is satisfied…does that make it bad? Not necessarily, because there is a give-and-take in any relationship, even in a sexual one. Maybe making sure that the other partner is fully satisfied the next time is the agreement, and it is worth them seeing their partner satisfied in the meantime…after all, in a relationship, shouldn't we be happy to see someone we love feeling good?

It takes effort and commitment on both parts to make each other happy sexually. Knowing your own body and what works is really important. Being able to masturbate or knowing your partner masturbates or helping them do so can be exciting and an adjunct to having sex. It is not a downfall, but a regular part of life that doesn't say anything about your ability to satisfy them. It doesn't have to be hidden or seen as shameful, but rather shows that they are still alive and vital sexually.

Nothing (short of health problems) stops a couple from having a happy and healthy sex life well into their 80's, even their 90's…doesn't that sound like a goal to work towards together? Bodies age, but imagination and creativity don't. Keep the lines of communication open and be open-minded. Knowing each other and our own bodies only helps to make things even better!

Chapter 9: Spirituality

Just like every aspect of life, people's needs for spirituality may change over time. The advent of children, losses of loved ones, the business of everyday life can all affect our commitment to our spiritual side. For some, it is a critical part of their identity, of who they are. For others, they maintain it without necessarily attending outside places of worship. Nevertheless, you both knew where you stood as spiritual individuals when you met…has that changed?

Sometimes, people get so busy in their lives that they don't have or make the time to attend places of worship, but having children makes them realize the importance of maintaining the commitment that they were raised with. Surely you discussed what religion the kids were to be raised in, but who is to maintain it? Hopefully, there is a mutually agreed-upon place that perhaps compromises to meet everyone's needs. The extended sense of family that a religious community can provide serves to reinforce the values and beliefs you want your children to embrace. One member may not feel as comfortable there, so maybe it takes some searching to find the right one for you both to feel comfortable…

Just like health, finances, emotional needs and sexual needs change over time with each individual, the same goes for their spiritual needs. A family member may have passed away to cause one of you to reach out to your religious community more and that is fine. Support them in their search for comfort and answers. A financial loss may have shaken another's faith, causing them to back away from their community. Be patient. Each in their own time and their own way.

What if your partner's beliefs or commitment have changed so much that you can't seem to fit with each other spiritually anymore?

Perhaps some time with your pastor or religious leader will help to clarify things together. What if your partner has not only withdrawn from your mutual faith, but turned to another? Be willing to listen and at least try it out, to see what has drawn them to it. You may be surprised. After all, however we name our higher power, all religions have him or her in common.

Patience, to hear each other out and really listen to what each other's faith means to them is paramount. Showing the respect for how you each think and what you feel is again so very important. Be honest about how you feel, don't harbor resentment or fear because that leads to further misunderstanding. What you don't know, ask and don't make assumptions. Trust in each other and in a higher power, if you believe, to help you work it out. And remember, people change over time in every way. It is a given, just like water flows...acceptance and listening will help you understand each other and be able to work together in your spiritual life, just like in every other aspect of your lives. Again, talking to a spiritual advisor can often help to clarify and work through any differences that may have emerged over time.

Chapter 10: You've tried it all and can't take it any longer
(There's no "best" age for the kids to survive this best)

Sadly, you've tried to work through your differences and there feels like there's no going back. Maybe someone has done something to break the trust and faith in the relationship, maybe you've just "fallen out of love" and try-as-you-might, can't seem to get it back. If you've tried counseling, seen your spiritual advisor, talked to your friends or family for suggestions to make things better, you've gone on a romantic trip together to get the spark back and nothing seems to work, do you still love each other? Is it enough?

Is it better to stay together "for the kids' sake", or can it be as harmful for them? All I can say is that kids use their parents' relationships as a template for their own in the future. Don't we all think of our parents' marriages (for good or bad) when we think of getting married? Do we really want the kids to see a cold, distant relationship where their parents don't laugh or hug or seem to enjoy each other's company? Do we really want them to know that their parents are staying together in misery because of them? That's a big burden for any kid to carry.

If you've mutually made the decision that separating is the best option, live with the decision for a while before acting on it and telling the kids. See if either of your feelings change, thinking of living apart from each other and from the kids for varying periods of time. If you feel wistful and find yourselves sad at the prospect while sitting around the dinner table sharing your kids' stories with them, talk to each other about it. Don't be rash. If you can, talk about options for the living situation, to make it as seamless and stable as possible for the kids. All of this assumes you are being two rational adults about this…

After all, it is not often a mutual decision to separate. Often, it is one member of the couple who wants out. Anyone knows that the party who wanted to keep on trying is going to be hurting more. Love is a power dynamic: the one who loves more stands to lose more, and the one who loves less has more power. Maybe the one who wants out was hurting a lot before and has gone through the grieving process on their own, without letting their partner know. That can feel very unfair and dishonest, as it never gave them a chance to work on things when their partner was still committed. Any which way you look at, this is a painful process.

Above all, I have to be very directive here and insist that no one starts looking to fill their partner's shoes before the decision has been mutually made to split and you've been apart for a while. If you really want to shelter you kids from as much hurt as possible, don't do it!!! It is hard enough for kids to see their parents with new partners, other than Mom or Dad, after the split has been formally done. Give them some dignity, some grace time to deal with it and digest the new situation. Don't be selfish. You chose to have children together and should care enough to lessen their pain. It will hurt more than enough to have their parents apart.

If you can, do an honest evaluation of where you are at financially or with an advisor. Remember, you don't want your kids suffering more than emotionally if at all possible. Being able to live comfortably with both parents will ease the strain. If they see a discrepancy, they will be caught in loyalties to one or the other and that's not fair to each other or to them.

If you absolutely can't agree on finances and/or feel that someone is not being honest, you have to protect yourself legally. Two people with two jobs/careers is one matter, but what if one has given up their career to stay home with kids? That complicates things even further, if the job-market has passed them by and they have to re-train or get more education. It can create a huge financial disparity between the two households.

It goes without saying that you loved each other once and truly cared about each other's well-being. Even with all of the hurt feelings, wouldn't you think that it would be fair to give each of you a fighting chance to succeed on your own? Should the hurt you're both feeling translate into even worse hurt and resentment towards each other in the future? Don't you both deserve happiness, even if it isn't as the couple you pictured yourselves together for the rest of your lives?

It's time to grow up and be adults. You're not little kids who have to sling mud at each other to get each other back. You made this life together, now it's time to figure out how to separate your lives from each other maturely. Get counseling if you can, each of you, to be able to incorporate this change into your lives personally. Maybe even see someone together. Try to think clearly before you dig yourselves into a quagmire of anger and resentment that you can't dig yourselves out of.

As we all know, once something is said, it's impossible to take back. Loving words are remembered and cherished, but mean, hurtful words can often replace them in one's more recent memory. Your partner is, after all, the mother/father of your children together. Your child or children carry half of their genetic make-up. Even if you can't think of it now, there are some good parts about your partner that they carry. Don't throw that away with mean-spirited comments.

And I can't reiterate enough…connecting with a new partner just complicates things and makes them worse. Yes, it may feel good for you in the short-term of hurt, but how does it help things as you prepare to separate? Does it feel better to know that your caring was transferred to someone else? In other words, isn't it better to work things through with each other first, without adding in the anger, resentment and indignity for your soon-to-be ex-partner of being displaced? I don't know whether it feels better for someone to know that their partner fell out-of-love with them or that they fell in love with someone else. There is hurt any which way, but I can't think that adding in the anger of someone else in the mix doesn't serve to fuel and drive things more in a negative direction.

Just as I have repeatedly stressed the importance of communication throughout a relationship, communication needs to continue to happen throughout this process. If talking with each other isn't an option because of tensions or hurts, try writing to each other to keep the lines of communication open. Being honest about what you're doing and respectful of each other's feelings remains equally important. We know the trust has been broken, because somewhere along the way, one or both of you was not on the same page while the other may have been merrily plowing along in the direction you forged together. Understand that: they feel misguided and cheated from the path they thought you were working towards together. Be kind, friendly if possible, even if just for the kids.

I am forever amazed at the couples who are able to remain friends after a split. Yes, it does happen! Maybe not right away, but over time. They have gotten over the bitterness and hurt and see that maybe they're better friends now than they were as a couple. My biggest watch-word for couples who are splitting is to try to at least be friendly. They may never be able to be the friends that I have seen some couples develop into, but if it's over, how does it serve anyone to hate each other to the end? Maintaining those negative feelings towards each other wastes and traps your energy to move on and forward to something better.

The bottom line is that something that you created together has died and one or both of you is grieving the loss. Just as losing someone we love who has died, we remember them for the good things, the wonderful experiences we shared with them. That is how we get on with living again. Just as we tried to have you look at your good shared memories earlier on, now is the time to reminisce (even just for yourself) about the good times you shared. Yes, it is bittersweet because the future is not together in the same way, but no one can take away memories, good or bad. Be grateful to each other for what you accomplished together: even looking at your children, remember they wouldn't be who they are without your partner!

Chapter 11: A child's perspective: Why are you ruining my life?

If at all possible, make sure that the kids don't hear about your troubles from someone else...in a phone conversation you're having with a friend that they can overhear or from their friends whose parents are your friends. Don't let them hear you arguing with each other about it while they're in their beds at night. Again, you brought them into this world together, why would you want to cause them more pain?

Try to sit down with each other and plan out how and when you're going to tell the kids. If one of you "jumps the gun" and tells them in advance, it will only serve to polarize them more. It is unfair to them and the other partner. You may have different versions of why you are separating but try to simplify things so that they aren't confused or upset with too much information. How you explain it will depend upon the kids' ages and maturity level. Remember though, kids are smart! They may have already seen it coming and have their own understanding of what has happened. Be respectful of their feelings and need for answers. The more straightforward and well-thought-out your plans are, the less worries they may have for their future. Remember, this is a huge loss for them, a death of something they thought they could count on: an intact family. They were born into it and are losing the security and protection it gave them from the outside world.

Hopefully, you will have already talked about a new potential living situation. Don't, for goodness sake, tell the kids the night someone is moving out. The feeling of loss is enough for the kids without the trauma of seeing the physical move of one parent out of the home. No doubt, you will already have talked about how you are planning to do this before talking to them.

Living Situation

Some people seem to be able to still live in the same home while separated, some for economic reasons, some to lessen the upset of change for the kids. If you can still be civil to each other and this works, more power to you...If this not an option, then maybe one of you moves to a place nearby while the other remains in the family home. Being close may not be ideal for you, but for the kids it keeps them in their family home. Some couples choose an option (and of course, this is when shared-parenting is mutually decided upon) where they have the apartment or other home close by and they rotate between the two places, each living with the kids in the family home and then rotating back to the other place when it's the other parent's turn.

What if your financial situation makes it very hard to keep the family home? Another option is to both buy smaller homes in the same area, again keeping the kids in their comfort zone (if not their home, at least their neighborhood where friends and schools are nearby). As much as an upheaval it is for them, you can both involve the kids in the process of searching out the new homes, choosing their bedrooms and helping decorate. It makes them feel part of the process in a good way.

What if the financial situation is in contention, with one of you having to "bunk-in" until things are settled at a friend's while the other remains in the home? A tricky situation and very stressful for all involved. The best you can do is not get the kids involved in the struggles and make the best of the situation...hopefully with visits at the family home or at extended family's if they live in town.

Positive Communication

Let's discuss what to talk about with the kids and what not to talk about. One of the most damaging things I have ever heard a parent say to their child is: "you're just like your mother/father". Think about it...you and the other parent are split and may not see each other as particularly likeable for some time anyways. Telling your child that he or she is like them evokes: "You are divorcing/are separated from Mom/Dad. Obviously, there are things you don't like about them or you'd stay together...what, are you going to divorce me now?!". Of course, your children have traits from each of you. Each of you has a combination of things you or they like and things you or they don't. How unfair to put that on a child! Don't do it!!!

When it comes to shared, individual time with each parent, let's not make it a secret. In other words, encourage your child to talk about their time with the other parent without criticizing. Don't say: "Oh, and how did they have the money to do that with you?" or belittle their efforts. Let it be okay to love and have fun with the other parent. They are a part of them, too. I have observed a phenomenon some call "splitting", where children in a split situation almost visually seem to switch at the halfway point between the two homes and cut off the part of their lives with the one parent to the other. They do it to cope with the strain of negativity that they feel runs when they return from the other parent. It is damaging and hurtful. Don't force them to feel they have to be two separate kids in two different lives. They didn't choose for you to split, you did. They shouldn't have to feel guilty for loving you both.

Making it Work in Two Homes

There are complications with children living in two homes…keeping up friendships, school-work, extra-curricular activities, among others. School success is critical to every child and our efforts as parents to help them with keeping up are so important. This is where perhaps a communication book between the two of you, to outline homework done or due, outstanding assignments or field-trips can be so helpful. Making sure that the school sends both of you copies of notices, report cards, permission slips, and parent-teacher meetings can really reduce frustrations. Maybe one of you is better at math or English, so that when assignments are due, the kids would prefer to have that parent helping them. Be fair to them and try to accommodate the best you can by being willing to compromise time. Parent-teacher meetings are always crucial to keeping up with our children's progress academically, socially and emotionally, especially at this time when their lives are turned upside-down. If you can be civil with each other, attend them together…if not, see the teacher(s) separately to ensure you're on the same page.

Maintaining friendships is so important for children at all times. Try to ensure that your kids keep up with their play-dates and/or sleep-overs with friends. They are a bridge to both homes. Don't feel that friend-time takes away from your time with them. As they get older, friends will naturally become more important to them…not because they don't want to spend time with you, but they have more in common with their friends. Friends are also a source of support.

If you can, keep the kids involved in their extra-curricular activities, whether classes or sports or groups. Again, it normalizes their lives and keeps them occupied in things that they enjoy. You both need to know their schedules for events, classes, recitals, practices and games. If attending events together is too uncomfortable, then sit apart but try not to block the other parent from being a part of your children's lives.

When it comes to sharing the kids, of course things are more complicated than when you lived together. But they are not a commodity. Don't take it upon yourself to account for every minute you are "due" of time with them. Let it be a natural give-and-take...sometimes they may need more Mom or Dad time and it's important to listen to how they are feeling. If the kids feel guilty about spending time with a parent, they won't enjoy the time as much. Their needs and feelings deserve to be heard and respected.

Transitions

Transition times between the two residences can be tense or stressful. If you can't be civil at each other's homes, find a place that is neutral territory. If you can't stand to look at each other, have a mutually agreed-upon intermediary (maybe at a daycare, a day-home, a family friend) do the transition. When the kids arrive, know that they need a breather. Give them some space. Some parents find that the kids get edgy before or after the transition and it takes some time for them to settle in. Don't take it personally, as they are just adjusting themselves to a different setting.

Do encourage the kids to communicate with the other parent when they're at your home. Every child has different needs, but sometimes a nightly "tuck-in" phone call can allow them to share their day and settle in for the night. As already mentioned, if they need help with schoolwork, sometimes just a phone-call can be helpful to help steer them in the right direction on their homework. Give them their space and privacy. Don't listen in or comment on what you may have inadvertently heard of their call. It is their time with the other parent and doesn't have to be seen as time taken away from you. If they need a pep-talk or to talk things through about a friend situation with the other parent, give them that time. Begrudging it only creates anxiety and resentment.

Shared Events

Birthdays, religious holidays, school breaks, summer holidays now have to worked out, whereas before it way easier because you all lived together. What to do about birthday parties, for instance? If you are amicable enough that you can both be there and plan it together or let one plan and you both pay your share, then do it! It makes kids feel great if their parents can still see their way clear to being friendly on their special day. If you can't, however, then some parents have two birthday parties…maybe some friends come to one and some the other or they all come to both. Whatever it takes to make your child's birthday positive and special for them, do it!

Sometimes it takes drawn-up custodial arrangements to split up the holidays (winter break, spring break, summer holidays) and it certainly complicates matters. Again, if you can share a special event together like opening presents Christmas morning or going to a special event with your religious community together, then go ahead, because it takes away a lot of confusion for the kids. But if you can't, be fair and rotate yearly Christmas Eve and Christmas morning (for example) or make one or the other your special time you celebrate. The same goes with spring and summer breaks…maybe one of you manages to figure out a holiday away with the kids for a week during their week with the kids. Wouldn't it be a great sign of commitment to the kids for the other parent to switch weeks?

With respect to sporting and other extra-curricular activities, it's great when both parents can support the kids by attending things. It doesn't mean you have to sit together. Let them see that you both support them and enjoy watching their endeavors. Don't make it awkward or anxious for them knowing that you'll be out there. Let them revel in having both parents who love them cheering them on.

New Traditions

Taking kids out of their comfort zone of what they know and expect can be very scary for them. The old traditions aren't the same without both parents there. Why not create new traditions for holidays that they only do with you? Maybe one of you is an avid skier and the other isn't...how about going skiing together on a winter break when you've never done it with them before? Or how about taking them to help at a soup kitchen over the break, to share their time with others less fortunate? Maybe neither of you has as much money to spare as before (which is often the case), how about making presents together or decorations for the new house?

Maybe trips away become too expensive...how about taking the kids camping and making that a new thing you do together? How about taking up a new hobby together, like building bird-houses or learning to cook together? It's all about the shared experiences with the kids, the time together making new memories...not how much money you spend.

Our world today is a wonderfully multicultural one, and there are so many wonderful traditions out there from all religions and cultures to share with our children. This gives you the opportunity to share more of yourselves from your own personal history that you may not have shared with them before. It gives them new experiences and increases their pride in who they are and what makes them a part of you.

New Partners

I have alluded to the timing of introducing someone new into your children's lives, being compassionate about letting them settle into the changes that have already happened. If you do start dating and meeting potential new partners, please take the kids' feelings into account. They will find it hard to see you with someone else other than their other parent. I almost guarantee that.

The rule-of-thumb is to wait 6 months into a relationship before introducing the new partner to the kids. That way, you have some stability in the relationship and may be more certain that they are the "one". For children having gone through losing their parents as a couple, they don't need to meet and try to connect with someone who you're not sure is going to be in your life on an ongoing basis. They will already have potential attachment issues with someone new and may still be dealing with seeing their parents apart. Don't expect them to be thrilled about it and give it time.

What if the kids absolutely can't stand your new partner? That's a tricky question. Maybe pull back a little and don't insist on them spending time together. Spend your time with the kids apart from them for a while. Show them that their needs are important and you're listening to how they feel. At the same time, putting your personal life on hold can give the impression that they control you. It is a balancing act. We have all heard of situations where the kids refuse to spend time with the new partner and their parent and it puts that parent in a tough position of having to choose. There is no easy answer to this dilemma.

It may take some initiative on the new partner's part to reach out to the kids, to establish a different relationship with them and assure them that they are not trying to replace the other parent or to take on that role. I have seen some wonderful relationships develop between the kids and the new partner, who takes on a "big sister/big brother" or aunt/uncle or benevolent older supportive friend role. It is all up to how receptive the kids are, their ages, and how open the person is to take on the challenge. But it is so worth it in the long-run, to avoid impacting on the closeness between parent and child.

Communication!

Here we go again with me stressing the importance of communication between parents, but also with the kids. You need to listen to how they're feeling, to what they want and what they need. This is a very vulnerable time for them and knowing that you are there for them to listen without judgment can be such a huge advantage and relief for them. It is an opportunity for your relationship to grow. But avoid the pitfall of becoming friends with the kids...they're not ready for it. Don't let them be your dating coach, your confidante or buddy. They're going through enough of their own feelings without knowing that you're still upset over the split or having financial problems or having a hard time being alone. Those are adult issues that belong with the adults. Talk to your friends, your family, your counselor, but don't talk to the kids about it. They don't need to feel guilty over at the other house knowing that you're lonely or sad.

Chapter 12: Pitfalls and traps that make matters worse: The blame-game

We've already talked about sheltering the kids from your feelings of self-doubt, anger, sadness or vulnerability. At the same time, it's critical to shelter them from your anger and upset at the other parent. Remember, that's their Mom/Dad you're talking about!

Each of your versions of why the relationship didn't work may be the same, they may be different. Telling the kids why in a unified story is always best. Do they need to know the nitty-gritty details? Does someone have to look like the good guy/bad guy? How does that make it any easier for the kids? This is where you have to be able to put your feelings aside and focus on their feelings.

Even after the fact, when the family has physically split apart, you will probably have differences of opinion, and different ways of doing things. It's inevitable because if your communication wasn't great before the break, what's to make it better now? It takes hard work to maintain meaningful communication for the children's sakes. Don't let them hear you arguing on the phone or in person at transitions, or they will be forever anxious whenever there is any interaction between you two. It may be that email is the best solution to maintain contact, because it can be so much less emotional in how it comes across.

Just as you may disagree on the reason(s) for the split, you may disagree about how each of you is raising the kids. With the help of a parenting coordinator who is experienced in dealing with this type of conflict, both of you can air your concerns and goals regarding the kids with an objective mediator. There are many ways to relate to and encourage kids. No one way is perfect, and we already know that you are different people with different histories. How one of you does things and relates to the kids may work for that parent, while the other's relationship and style of parenting may work better for them. It is all a learning process to work together but independently in your children's best interests.

If there are disagreements financially, don't let the kids hear about it. They are already worried and anxious about how this is all going to work out. Deal with it as adults, not with or through the kids. They don't deserve to feel guilty because of expenses you incur with them. They already know that you both wouldn't have to interact if it wasn't for them...isn't that enough of a burden?

When or if a new partner comes onto the scene, don't make an issue of it with or through the kids. Give them the freedom to get to know this person if they want to. If you can, encourage them to give it a try. Getting your own feelings involved, of feeling displaced or replaced already complicates matters for the kids. They may not want to hurt, upset or disappoint you by being open to meeting or liking this person. If they have issues with this person, try not to get involved but empower them to talk to the other parent about it or to the new partner, themselves. It's part of the natural growing process to empower our children to deal with their issues with others on their own.

Remember that loyalty issues are inevitable...kids may side with one parent or against another parent. They may even choose not to engage with a new partner in their loyalty to the other parent. Assure them that it's okay to love both of you. Let them know that you don't feel it is disloyal or hurts you for them to get to know the other parent's new partner. If it does bother you so much, then you need some help to deal with it.

If you do have to move, retrain or go back to work, try to make it as positive an experience for the children as you can. Engage them in the challenge to do something new. Seeing their parents back in school or working is often a positive motivator for kids and doesn't have to be seen as a bad thing. It is a change, but how a person deals with change often depends upon how it is framed or explained to them. Moving to a new house or a new child-care setting because of work schedules can be scary, but they can also be exciting new opportunities.

Aside from the children, living your life blaming, resentful and angry about what might have been serves you no good. Similarly, self-blame only makes us feel worse. How can you make this unexpected turn-of-events into a positive? It's hard in the short-term but remember that you've survived through other upheavals in your life before. We all have. How did you manage to push through the pain and deal with the upset before? Did you turn to your support system? If so, reach out to them again. Did you get busy with focusing on what you needed to do? Then do that again. Did you go out there and try something new, challenge yourself outside of your comfort zone? Then do it again.

Everyone has her or his own ways of coping, the "habits" of going into survival mode. This is a pretty important time to not get into unhealthy habits that you may have turned to when life got you down in the past. By that, I mean alcohol, prescription medications, drugs, excessive shopping, jumping into multiple relationships, among others. You not only have yourself to worry about, you now have your children, as well. A healthy parent emotionally, physically, financially and in every way is what they need right now.

If you've been for counseling before, try it again to help you figure out how to deal with and incorporate this change into your life. If you haven't been before, consider at least trying it, to have an objective, empathic person outside of your family and friends to help you work this through. It doesn't help you or anyone else holding onto these feelings. Even if you project them outwards, towards your ex-, how does that help things in the long-run? There are ways of helping you to feel better. In a way, the faster and healthier you become, the less power you are giving your ex- to still impact on you. It frees you to get on with your own life and enjoy what is ahead of you with the energy to meet new challenges.

Chapter 13: Focus on the Children

You made the decision to have children. In so doing, you made a promise to them to nurture them, to love them, to keep them safe, to help them succeed, grow and mature. Now is a critical time in their lives that they really need you. I've already talked about how having a healthy parent is so important for your children's well-being. Now let's look at what they're going through.

Depending upon your child's age at the time of a marital split, he or she may be experiencing different things. Let's look at it developmentally...infants need to feel secure and comforted, their physical needs listened to and met. For an infant to go through a split, they need to feel that security and stability. They don't understand what is happening and it can be frightening for them. Parents need to work hard to ensure they feel safe. Change is hard for them. Being apart from a parent who they may be more attached to creates anxiety and upset. They may find it hard settling in with the other parent and every attempt to help them feel comfortable should be made. This is where the communication of meeting their needs is extremely important. If they like things done a certain way as they probably do, try your best to maintain the same feeding and sleep schedules. Give it time for them to adjust. If they are really distressed in the initial period of adjustment, work together if you can to make things the same in both homes as much as possible.

Toddlers are naturally inquisitive, and their temperaments start to show through more as they become more verbal. Listen to them. If they want to talk to the other parent, do it for them. It isn't a failure on your part. It is just how they feel. Helping them to feel comfortable and secure is again the watch-word. You will develop new and different relationships with them as they are able to express their needs more. Tantrums are a sign that they confused and filled with emotions they are having a difficult time expressing. Be patient. Don't blame them for how they feel. Find ways to help them feel better, to be able to comfort themselves. As for infants, often having "transitional objects", like stuffed animals, favorite blankets, pictures of the other parent in the other home are comforting to them. Make sure that you ensure these items are rotated back and forth between homes, as being without them can be very distressing.

Children have so much going on inside them and in their lives. Maintaining their school, extra-curricular and friendship networks helps keep them feeling settled. They need help to keep up with their school-work in both homes. As already mentioned, if one parent is "better" at a subject in school, let them reach out for help with this parent if it's not you. Bargaining in good faith in this way lets them know that above all, their needs are worth being met. Keeping them on the same teams or in the same classes helps in the same way, to give them a sense of continuity between the homes. Encouraging and maintaining the same and new friendships gives them the support system all kids need and normalizes what's going on in their life.

For teenagers, who generally have a very well-established social life, ensure that you do your best to help accommodate them. Remember that time with their friends doesn't have to be seen as time apart from you. They need their friends and it is not a competition for their attention. Even if you were both still together, your teenager would probably be spending more time with friends than at home. If you notice they're becoming less social or withdrawing, just like for younger children, make note of it. Talk to them about it to make sure they're feeling okay. Sometimes withdrawal from others and the outside world are symptoms of upset and/or depression. Try to help them work it through and if it doesn't help, seek outside help from counseling. The adjustment can be hard.

There are numerous issues to consider when dealing with children of all ages: attachment issues, separation issues, social/academic issues, health issues, sibling relationships, among a host of others. Kids go through attachment, or feeling connected and close, often on a rotating basis between parents even if they are still together. Parents being separate and living apart can really challenge this attachment if they're not feeling as secure with one of the parents at a particular time. Be sensitive to these feelings and really listen. Help them to feel as comfortable with each of you. It is not a competition as to who is the better parent. If at all possible, kids need their mothers and their fathers in their lives and helping each other for the kids' sakes in this regard is a selfless and loving act. Be encouraging along with the other parent to try and meet their needs and encourage the kids to express how they feel and what they need from that parent.

Separation anxiety results from feelings of distress when apart from a securely attached person in a child's life. In other words, if a child normally would have a bed-time story or snuggling time with one parent and they are at the other's home, it can be very distressing to them. Listen to how they're feeling. Encourage them to have that phone-call before bed-time with the other parent. Try to establish your own way of meeting these needs, maybe with your own bedtime routine you create together or try to maintain the same at your home. If one parent has tended to be the comforter when the kids are sick or hurt, try your best to help them feel better in the same way. If you can't help them, reach out to the other parent to help out. Show them that you're listening to their needs. If they're having a really hard time with being in one home, apart from the parent they are more attached to, do your best to work together to make adjustments and make it better. Again, it is not about your needs or the other parent's needs, it is about the kids'. They didn't ask for this huge change in their lives. Help them try to feel the best they can in both homes.

With regards to school, remember that with so much new going on in their lives, some kids may have a harder time focusing at school. Trying to concentrate when they're still trying to figure out which home they're going home to, which parent is picking them up, who is going to help them with their homework, can be tough. Keep in close touch with teachers to see how children are doing. Some may show no changes at all, others may be having a hard time. Working with the teacher together, giving and listening to suggestions can only make things better.

School is not only academic. It is also a highly social place for kids. They hopefully have a support system of friends there. Having friends who may have been through the same thing, whose parents have also separated, can be a very normalizing and empowering experience for kids. If a friend has successfully made it through their parents splitting, it gives comfort to a child who is just beginning the process. Years ago, when fewer or no parents may have split, it would have been quite a lonely experience for a child who is the only one in a separate living situation. Sharing similar experiences can be extremely comforting, knowing that others have made it through okay.

As with any other change in life, there can be an impact on one's health. If you notice changes in your child's eating or sleep habits, any weight loss or gain, any changes in their behavior or interest in activities, talk to your doctor. Make sure that both of you are in contact and attend/or with the physician for regular check-ups. Keeping up with children's health should be an issue with for both of you and sharing information with each other with regards to their health, just like their education, is in a child's best interests. If your physician has suggestions or concerns, work together in both homes to address them. You created your children together, shouldn't you work together to ensure they are as happy and healthy as they can be?

When you have more than one child together, there are siblings to help each other out. In any family, there are bound to be issues between siblings, because they're different people. Helping siblings to get along and support each other during this time can make a big difference. An older brother or sister can often help a younger one to feel and understand better. Having someone else there who is sharing in the changes can be very helpful. It can often bring them closer as they try to figure things out together. Encourage them to support each other. If they didn't get along too well before, they may relate to each other better now. Conversely, they could be more at-odds because of the stress of the situation. Be understanding and try to help them to work out their differences, to be there for each other.

I cannot underscore how important it is to ensure that your child does not feel responsible for your separation. Even if they don't say it, many kids feel that they were enough of a "problem" that it helped create the rift between you two. Of course, parents sometimes argue or disagree about the kids, but it it's never enough to cause a couple to separate. Make sure that your children know that it wasn't their fault. They need to know that it had nothing to do with them, that being apart is to make things better for everyone.

Just as not feeling they were the cause of the split, kids need to know that it is not their job to get you back together. I have seldom spoken to a youngster whose biggest wish and dream is for their parents to get back together again, for their family to be whole once more. Some may try their best to create situations where you are together, hoping that it will make things right. If they know that one partner pulled out first, they may plead for the other parent, to let them know that there is still love there and not to give up. It is their desperation to try to make things "right". Listen to them and both reassure them that you both still love them, that your love for each other helped create the special person that they are and that is something that you will always have between you.

Consider the complication of your children's lives now between two homes. If you grew up in the security of one home, think how much more confusing it can be for them trying to live their lives in two places...two rooms, two sets of clothes, perhaps two sets of rules, maybe two different child-care situations and schedules. Life is not so simple anymore. I remember talking to one child years ago who explained that the only way they could remember which home they were returning to at the end of the day was by what they had eaten for breakfast that day. It does have a huge impact on their lives.

If you grew up in two homes, then you can empathize and help them figure things out but it is still something they have never experienced. Try to help them deal with the transitions, the exchange of important information and things between homes. Do your best to make it as easy as possible for them. For older children, it is a little easier than for the younger ones as they can plan things out a little better. For a child who may be disorganized or still really upset by the change in situation, it can be nightmare. The more you can help out and encourage them, the easier it will be for them to adapt.

Always remember that it may have been your decision to separate, but you are not the only ones impacted by that decision. Even if you are relieved or devastated in the aftermath, your children feel everything, too. They need your compassion and your help to get through this tough time. Watch them, listen to them and help them understand that you will make it through this together. Their family may be different now, but it is still a family of a different sort. Help them appreciate and enjoy what may be two tension-free homes now, without the conflict between parents. Encourage them to be happy with each parent, that it is okay to feel better and enjoy time with each of you. If you can, share special times with them. If you can't, do your best to shelter them from further conflict. They have seen and experienced enough. Let them get on with the experience of being kids, not "children of divorce".

Chapter 14: The Aftermath: Consolidation and Growth

Working through the multitude of issues and feelings in the course of a marital split is no easy task. It is hard, to say the least, and challenges you to address issues about yourself, your relationships and your future that you'd never have thought you had to even think about. It makes you look at yourself, your values and beliefs, your hopes and dreams, your strengths and weaknesses, things you may never have even questioned because you felt secure about them. Sometimes it takes tough situations to bring things into focus, to challenge what we have known and accepted. That is not necessarily a bad thing.

People can always grow and change and sometimes it takes even a negative event to create that opportunity. It is how we frame or think about experiences that impacts on how we deal with them. Instead of seeing a marital separation as all negative for instance, see it as a chance to make a positive difference in your life. You may not agree at all with what your ex- said about you, but were there things you wanted to do, to change on your own? Now is your chance, unencumbered by their opinion.

Had you "always wanted to..." go back to school or redecorate the house to your taste? Had you thought of getting involved in some outside activity like a sport or salsa dancing or some craft but never felt like you could? Now is your chance to become who you want to be. Even the little things count...had you never done laundry in the morning because it was frowned upon? Now's your chance...did you stop cooking brussels sprouts because your ex- hated them? Now's your chance...did you stop exercising because the time you took for yourself was frowned upon? Now's your chance...did you cut back on outside friendships because your ex- didn't like them? Now's your chance...there is only you to answer to. It can be a very freeing (but also scary) experience, having the freedom to make decisions and change your life.

What did you learn from your marriage about yourself? Did you like who you became when you were in it? You can see it as a tremendous learning experience for possible future relationships. Are you the kind of person who "loses themselves" in a relationship, becoming so much a part of the couple that you forget yourself? Now is the time to develop a strong sense of you outside of a relationship, to be able to carry that forward into any relationships you may have in the future.

What did you learn about your friends or family through this process? Were they unconditionally supportive? In this situation, as in any stressful one, people can really show themselves to be supporters or not. Were your friends there for you? Did you lose some along the way? This is a tough one...some couple-friends can feel uncomfortable in a marital split and don't want to take sides. They may have been closer to one or the other or just don't want any part of it at all and pull away. It can really hurt, but isn't it good to know in a tough situation who your real friends are? It is also a real opportunity to meet new friends, maybe in other activities you join, with similar interests.

What did you learn about your finances? Were you both involved in working on your financial goals together? If not, with whatever is left of your joint and now divided "marital property", you are in charge. If it's a scary prospect, reach out for help from your financial institution or advisor to understand your situation and work towards achieving your new goals.

What have you learned about yourself as a parent? Have you been sensitive to your children, to help them through this? What changes have you made to your routines, your daily lives to compensate? Has it given you more or less time together? How have you accommodated to make things the best they can be? This is a challenge, to ensure the continued closeness and time spent with your children.

What about your relationship with your now ex- in-laws and extended family? How have the relationships changed, if at all? If you are in the fortunate position that they still respect you as the other parent of their grand-kids/nieces/nephews that goes a long way towards easing tensions. Still being treated with respect and dignity by your ex's family is a pleasant surprise because sometimes, "blood is thicker than water", as the saying goes. What if they pull away out of loyalty to their family member? How have you dealt with it? It may feel like a personal attack, but perhaps it is from confusion as to how to relate to you now. Is there some way to connect with them, to try and ease their worries, to let them know you understand? If tension still remains between you and their son/daughter/brother/sister, have you made an effort to maintain their relationship with the kids? Even if you are not as close right now, that may change over time as they sort things out. Helping your children maintain a relationship with their extended family is still very important.

What if your ex's friends or extended family try to involve the children in the issues? Adult issues are just that…adult issues. Children should not be drawn into them. This needs to be clarified and worked through with your ex- and/or their family. They need to be reminded that whether you are their family member or not, no matter how they feel, your children are still just that…part of you. You still deserve their respect as the mother/father of their grandchildren/nieces/nephews. Whether you still like each other or not, just as with your ex-, the relationship still remains because of your connection through the children.

Are you ready for a new relationship? Are your children ready for you to date or see other people? Only you can answer that. They may never be ready to see you with someone other than their father or mother. The children need to understand, however, that your happiness is important, too. What have you learned from your marriage to help you in new relationships? Do you know yourself better, what you need and what you want, who you are? Do you want someone in your life because it will enrich your life or because you're feeling lonely? Only you will know but filling an empty space before you're ready can lead to connecting with the wrong person for you in the long-run. Why?

The person who we are in the fray of loss, sadness and possibly anger and resentment is not who may really be. The face that we show the world is what attracts people to us. If you show the world a bitter, empty person, will that attract the same person who would fit with you when you are through this process? Think of pieces of a puzzle...they fit together filling in the holes from each shape. Whatever fits into the shape you present to the world may not be the same as what you present when you are feeling "whole" again. That can lead to further complications or confusion for yourself and/or your children later on...more about future relationships later.

So how can you come out of this turmoil a stronger, happier, healthier person? Now is the time to really be self-aware of where you are in life. It's the time to make the changes you may not have felt capable of doing before. You have an opportunity for a fresh start on life. Yes, there are challenges that may remain from the separation financially, emotionally, socially, maybe even physically, but you can make it work. You have to, for your children's sake and for your own.

Putting it all aside and just plowing through to survive and get on with things needs to happen in some regards but taking care of yourself to be able to live and enjoy life again is a goal that will benefit your whole family. Take time for yourself, to think things through or talk things through with friends or family, even a counselor if it's not working and you feel you're "stuck". Be patient with yourself. There's no time-table to feel better. Like any loss in our lives, every person works through things differently and in his or her own time. Just like any event in our lives, you will make it through to happiness on the other side. There's no rush. Sometimes, the road there is the most important lesson you will learn, seeing yourself rise to the challenge. You have made it through tough times before and you will again.

Chapter 15: New Relationships: Can you ever trust (yourself) again?

Maybe you're already in a new relationship, maybe you're contemplating one, maybe you're not sure if you're ready to start looking for one...how are you supposed to know if and when you're ready? As I already explained, there is no perfect time to know when you're "ready", but there are some signs that you may be by being honest with yourself about how you're really feeling.

Are you really "over" your ex-? Do you still have strong feelings of anger, resentment, remorse, sadness or any combination of them? If these feelings are still strong, you may be looking at the world through a different color of glasses. Seeing things clearly takes the ability to examine them both rationally and emotionally. You may be able to rationalize that you deserve to be happy in a new relationship and that's absolutely true, but are you approaching a new relationship with a clean slate emotionally?

I've already mentioned how what we present to the world of ourselves draws people to us. If you present an unhappy, resentful, bitter or hurting person, who will be attracted to that? You may find someone who is compassionate, entering into a care-giver role or someone who may have their own similar issues, but how is that going to help you get out of that state of mind? Having worked through all of the negative feelings about the past as much as possible (understanding that new situations may arise that are still upsetting), isn't that the person you want to show the world? Someone whole, optimistic, growing, confident and aware of themselves attracts similar people. Isn't that the kind of person you want in your life?

Do you still find yourself thinking a lot about your marriage and about your ex-? Are you able to remember the good times, to look at the balance of positives and negatives from your time together? Have you learned anything from the marriage? Can you see where things started to go "off" the path you had tried to create together? Are there things you could have or would do differently now?

Some of the biggest fears about entering into a new relationship involve the same dynamic happening again. We have already read about, heard of and seen people partnering with someone who is very similar to their ex-...how does this set you up for happiness and success in a new relationship? Then there are the people who partner with someone totally opposite of their ex-, perhaps hoping that someone totally different will make things better. But are you still the same person who was in the previous relationship? How have you grown and changed? Shouldn't that be taken into account when searching for another partner in life?

<u>Don't Rush It!</u>

Let's say you're feeling pretty good about yourself now and feel ready to be in a relationship. One of my familiar refrains with people is to stop looking and they'll be surprised when it happens. What that means is: being desperate to find someone may make us lower our expectations. Remember the joke about people at the end of the night in a club...everyone frantically partnering up with who isn't already taken? The house lights come up...look at who you're with...surprised?

It's not that I'm saying not to make yourself available or present yourself in situations to meet someone, but the flurry of rushing into something may result in a potentially wrong match. Certainly, staying at home and waiting for the phone to ring is not going to help things. Involving yourself in groups, clubs or activities that you really enjoy will expose you to people with similar interests, give you something in common. It's a great starting point. Maybe you've always wanted to take dance lessons but your ex- wasn't interested? There are great classes and clubs out there for singles to learn and mingle. Always wanted to learn a new sport? Again, there are always great clubs out there to try out and learn new skills and meet new people. You may even meet some great new friends in the process!

Try to enjoy your time out of the marriage. Learn to be alone without feeling lonely. Give yourself time to enjoy your own company. If you don't enjoy time with yourself, how is someone else going to? Catch up on the world around you...you've probably been so preoccupied with the stress of your situation, it's been hard to look outwards. Re-connect with old friends who you may have lost touch with or may have been waiting in the wings for you to call when you're ready. If your family is encouraging you to take a break and will look after the kids while you enjoy a "staycation" at home or away by a lake or on a beach, take them up on it. Give yourself the time you need to heal if you can. It's amazing what a fresh perspective on yourself and your life can show you.

Are the Kids Ready?

Now for the tough one...you may feel ready to think about a new relationship, but are your kids ready? Are they still hurting a lot, having problems accepting the separation? If they are, how can they be ready for a new partner? They will see the new person as competition for the other parent as they hope desperately that you will get back together. How will you know that they're ready? Talk to them and really listen to how they're feeling. Explain that you understand how they feel, but do they want to have a parent who feels happy and fulfilled, as well?

Hopefully, they've seen you trying new things, meeting new people, doing things that make you feel good and happier. It may even be a little scary for them seeing you changing over time. Understand that and help them understand that you are still the parent they have always known, but you are also a person in your own right. They may only see you as "Mom" or "Dad", and they may not have seen you as anything but that and a part of the couple that was their parents. While growth and change can be exciting for you, it can be confusing for them. Give them time to see a happier person, a happier parent and they will see that it can be better for them, as well. I have heard from many children that they feel better about things and happier to see both parents happy in their lives, not living in the tension that existed in the home before. They can enjoy their time in each home with each parent and despite the inherent complication of living in two homes, the quality of their lives in each is better.

Know that any new person in your and your children's lives will be compared to your ex-, by you and by them. For your kids, perhaps no one will ever "stack up" compared to their other parent. Assure them that they don't need to, that they are not replacing the other parent in their lives. A new, different person can enrich their lives and make yours happier and your happiness impacts well for them. Assure them that a new person is not replacing them, either and will not affect the quality of your time together. It can, if they are not used to you taking time away from them, but make sure that when you are together, it is the same dedicated parent-child time they always enjoyed.

As I already explained, it is really important not to "introduce" the kids to a new partner unless you can see the relationship being long-term, at least. Having already lost the security of the family situation from before, it can be very upsetting and confusing for them to try to bond with and appreciate someone new, only to lose another person from their lives if it doesn't work out.

Hopefully, your new partner is open to and interested in your children...in today's world, they may even have children of their own. Combining families, with children from two previous unions can be a wonderful addition for the kids but can also create jealousies about how your time is spent. Different parenting styles and the attitude your new partner has towards your children (and you towards his or hers) can create some potential sources of conflict or confusion. This is a path that needs good communication with each other, both before and as the relationships continue.

Comparisons with your Ex-

Just as the kids will make comparisons, so will you...are you ready to see someone new in their own light, not constantly comparing them to your ex-, whether favorably or not? After the end of any relationship, there are bound to be comparisons, but after a long-term marriage, it is too easy to refer back. When people say that there is "baggage" we bring along from previous relationships, that's exactly right. There is no question that we learn from every experience, every relationship we've been in, hence the reason for dating and getting to know a variety of potential partners before we choose one. But do we constantly have to measure this new person by the infamous "ex-"?

Each person is an individual in his or her own right, with their own history and experiences. Making a potential new partner "pay the price" for what happened with your ex- is unfair. It's your issue, not theirs. Every person brings along potential "baggage" from any previous relationship. Just because yours was a long-standing marriage is no different. A new relationship needs a clean slate, unencumbered by the faults of your previous partner. If there are already too many similarities between your new potential partner and your ex-, be honest with yourself if you can see past it. The earlier part of a relationship is all about deciding if you can accept the things that irritate you or whether they will continue to be a problem. The same goes for warning signs that remind you of your ex-…if it continues to plague you, you may not be ready yet to enter into a new relationship or it may be the wrong person. Like in any relationship, communicate with your new partner along the way, don't harbor resentments and let things fester.

Keeping your new Partner out of the Conflict

Let's say you've found someone who you want to share yours and your children's lives with…good for you! Yet another pitfall to avoid is involving him or her too much in the ongoing issues with your ex-. The reasons for this are two-fold: would you want to live your life continually hearing complaints from a new partner about a past relationship? Doesn't a new relationship deserve to begin with a positive focus on each other, not a past partner? The other problem that I have often seen happen is that the new partner gets "on the band-wagon" with fanning the flames of discontent with the ex-. Being supportive is one thing, but sometimes the new partner can get too involved and drive the tension even further. At the end of the day, the issue is between the two members of the ex-couple, not to be complicated by new significant others. Encouragement to be assertive is a far cry from driving an even greater wedge between two people who already have issues.

New Relationships and your Ex-

What if your ex- has problems with you being in a new relationship? What if they don't "like" this person and have an issue with him or her being with the kids? First things first, we all know that it can be hard to see an ex- with someone else, especially if they're doing the things together that you had always wanted to do. Seeing him or her happy with someone else can be hurtful, particularly for the one who may have wanted to keep trying in the marriage. Remember, it is rare for two people to decide at the same time that the relationship is over. One is inevitably more hurt than the other and it's usually the one who still has more feeling for the other. Try to be kind. Don't flaunt the relationship but if you can give your ex- some advanced notice that the kids may be talking about someone new in their lives, it can avoid the added indignity of surprise. Spare your children being the harbingers of the news. It's not fair to them.

Your ex- may have gotten over the fact that you are in a new relationship or may also be in a new one themselves. A further possible complication is if he or she has issues with your new partner. It may simply be that they don't like them (they don't have to like them, you chose not to stay together, after all), or they may have what they see as valid concerns. No, your ex- has no right to rule your life or your choices of who you want to live your life with, but they do have a say when it comes to the kids. Hear them out…what is it that troubles them about this person with regards to the children? Does he or she have their own children? Have they never had children? Are there confrontations with him or her around or about the kids?

Understand that there is bound to be some competition or jealousy of another male or female in your house-hold who your ex- may see as taking his or her place. That should not be allowed to happen, as your ex- is still the mother or father of your children together. Try to ensure and assure that the newly-developing relationship with your children is not taking the other parent's place. And a really important piece of this new puzzle of new relationships is to keep the kids out of it. Putting down your ex-'s new partner is not okay and places the children in a tough situation of divided loyalties. I always believe that we should vote for those who show us what they can do, not those who focus on what the other isn't doing. Show the kids the parent you can be. Don't focus on what your ex- or their new partner isn't doing.

Establishing a New, Healthy Relationship

Just as we examined the parts of a healthy relationship/marriage, this new one needs to establish its own style of communication, trust, honesty and respect. Make sure to keep the lines of communication open...express yourself and be willing to listen. Ensure that this new beginning starts out right with clear expectations. Be honest about how you feel and what you want and encourage your new partner to be honest with you. Don't let things fester over time...we have seen what that does over time in your previous relationship. Be respectful and expect respect from your new partner...it is so crucial to feeling that they really care about who you are and what you want from life.

Trust can be a tough one to develop after the break-up of a long-time relationship. For whatever reason the marriage didn't work, and there are inevitably "trust issues" that remain, whether financially, emotionally, sexually or in any number of areas. Be honest about what bothers you and creates this insecurity for you. If you don't ask, you'll never know and then fears, resentments and insecurities may build up again.

You can find love again, but you need to know and love yourself first. You are wiser for having made it through …bruised, of course, but there is light at the end of that tunnel. You will learn to trust yourself and someone else again. It takes hard work to get yourself to a place where you are open to someone new in your life. Don't rush it. Choose to be open to someone because you're ready, not because you're lonely or can't bear to be alone again. You're worth far more than that. Jumping into a relationship before you're ready interferes with your time to really get to know yourself again. Don't you and your kids deserve that…a person/parent who feels fulfilled and ready to enhance their lives with new love? They want you to be happy. It impacts on their own happiness, too.

That new, healthy relationship should be with yourself, as well. You've been challenged by a profound loss in your life as a couple. But we also know that from loss comes new growth. It takes a lot of hard work to regain some sense of "normalcy" as a person again. You've learned from it, grown and changed in the process, and gotten to know yourself better. You've come to an understanding of your own wants and needs, as well as how to meet them and that shouldn't take someone else to meet them. This is your chance to find you again, an even better, stronger, and happier version.

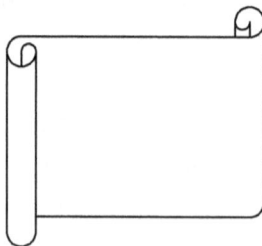

www.ingramcontent.com/pod-product-compliance
Lightning Source LLC
Chambersburg PA
CBHW070549030426
42337CB00016B/2422